THEME:

☐ FANTASY ☐ ~~SYMBOLS~~

☐ NIGHTMARE ☐ RANDOM

WHAT HAPPENED?

RECURRING? ☐ YES ☐ NO

FINAL THOUGHTS/INTERPRETATION:

THEME: **DATE:**

☐ FANTASY   ☐ SYMBOLIC

☐ NIGHTMARE   ☐ RANDOM

WHAT HAPPENED?

RECURRING? ☐ YES ☐ NO

FINAL THOUGHTS/INTERPRETATION:

THEME: **DATE:**

☐ FANTASY   ☐ SYMBOLIC

☐ NIGHTMARE   ☐ RANDOM

WHAT HAPPENED?

RECURRING? ☐ YES ☐ NO

FINAL THOUGHTS/INTERPRETATION:

THEME:　　　　　　　　　　**DATE:**

☐ FANTASY　　　☐ SYMBOLIC

☐ NIGHTMARE　　☐ RANDOM

WHAT HAPPENED?

RECURRING? ☐ YES ☐ NO

FINAL THOUGHTS/INTERPRETATION:

THEME: **DATE:**

☐ FANTASY   ☐ SYMBOLIC

☐ NIGHTMARE   ☐ RANDOM

WHAT HAPPENED?

RECURRING? ☐ YES ☐ NO

FINAL THOUGHTS/INTERPRETATION:

THEME: **DATE:**

- [ ] FANTASY   [ ] SYMBOLIC
- [ ] NIGHTMARE   [ ] RANDOM

WHAT HAPPENED?

RECURRING? [ ] YES [ ] NO

FINAL THOUGHTS/INTERPRETATION:

THEME: **DATE:**

☐ FANTASY   ☐ SYMBOLIC

☐ NIGHTMARE   ☐ RANDOM

WHAT HAPPENED?

RECURRING? ☐ YES ☐ NO

FINAL THOUGHTS/INTERPRETATION:

THEME: **DATE:**

☐ FANTASY   ☐ SYMBOLIC

☐ NIGHTMARE   ☐ RANDOM

WHAT HAPPENED?

RECURRING? ☐ YES ☐ NO

FINAL THOUGHTS/INTERPRETATION:

THEME: **DATE:**

☐ FANTASY   ☐ SYMBOLIC

☐ NIGHTMARE   ☐ RANDOM

WHAT HAPPENED?

RECURRING? ☐ YES ☐ NO

FINAL THOUGHTS/INTERPRETATION:

THEME: **DATE:**

☐ FANTASY ☐ SYMBOLIC

☐ NIGHTMARE ☐ RANDOM

WHAT HAPPENED?

RECURRING? ☐ YES ☐ NO

FINAL THOUGHTS/INTERPRETATION:

THEME: **DATE:**

☐ FANTASY   ☐ SYMBOLIC

☐ NIGHTMARE   ☐ RANDOM

WHAT HAPPENED?

RECURRING? ☐ YES ☐ NO

FINAL THOUGHTS/INTERPRETATION:

THEME: **DATE:**

☐ FANTASY   ☐ SYMBOLIC

☐ NIGHTMARE   ☐ RANDOM

WHAT HAPPENED?

RECURRING? ☐ YES ☐ NO

FINAL THOUGHTS/INTERPRETATION:

THEME: **DATE:**

☐ FANTASY   ☐ SYMBOLIC

☐ NIGHTMARE   ☐ RANDOM

WHAT HAPPENED?

RECURRING? ☐ YES ☐ NO

FINAL THOUGHTS/INTERPRETATION:

THEME: **DATE:**

☐ FANTASY   ☐ SYMBOLIC

☐ NIGHTMARE   ☐ RANDOM

WHAT HAPPENED?

RECURRING? ☐ YES ☐ NO

FINAL THOUGHTS/INTERPRETATION:

THEME: **DATE:**

☐ FANTASY   ☐ SYMBOLIC

☐ NIGHTMARE   ☐ RANDOM

WHAT HAPPENED?

RECURRING? ☐ YES ☐ NO

FINAL THOUGHTS/INTERPRETATION:

THEME: **DATE:**

☐ FANTASY   ☐ SYMBOLIC

☐ NIGHTMARE   ☐ RANDOM

WHAT HAPPENED?

RECURRING? ☐ YES ☐ NO

FINAL THOUGHTS/INTERPRETATION:

THEME: **DATE:**

☐ FANTASY   ☐ SYMBOLIC

☐ NIGHTMARE   ☐ RANDOM

WHAT HAPPENED?

RECURRING? ☐ YES ☐ NO

FINAL THOUGHTS/INTERPRETATION:

THEME: **DATE:**

☐ FANTASY   ☐ SYMBOLIC

☐ NIGHTMARE   ☐ RANDOM

WHAT HAPPENED?

_____
_____
_____
_____
_____
_____
_____
_____
_____
_____
_____
_____
_____
_____
_____
_____
_____
_____
_____
_____
_____
_____

RECURRING? ☐ YES ☐ NO

FINAL THOUGHTS/INTERPRETATION:

THEME: **DATE:**

☐ FANTASY ☐ SYMBOLIC

☐ NIGHTMARE ☐ RANDOM

WHAT HAPPENED?

RECURRING? ☐ YES ☐ NO

FINAL THOUGHTS/INTERPRETATION:

THEME: **DATE:**

☐ FANTASY   ☐ SYMBOLIC

☐ NIGHTMARE   ☐ RANDOM

WHAT HAPPENED?

RECURRING? ☐ YES ☐ NO

FINAL THOUGHTS/INTERPRETATION:

THEME: **DATE:**

- [ ] FANTASY [ ] SYMBOLIC
- [ ] NIGHTMARE [ ] RANDOM

WHAT HAPPENED?

RECURRING? [ ] YES [ ] NO

FINAL THOUGHTS/INTERPRETATION:

THEME: **DATE:**

☐ FANTASY   ☐ SYMBOLIC

☐ NIGHTMARE   ☐ RANDOM

WHAT HAPPENED?

RECURRING? ☐ YES ☐ NO

FINAL THOUGHTS/INTERPRETATION:

THEME: **DATE:**

☐ FANTASY   ☐ SYMBOLIC

☐ NIGHTMARE   ☐ RANDOM

WHAT HAPPENED?

RECURRING? ☐ YES ☐ NO

FINAL THOUGHTS/INTERPRETATION:

THEME: **DATE:**

☐ FANTASY   ☐ SYMBOLIC

☐ NIGHTMARE   ☐ RANDOM

WHAT HAPPENED?

RECURRING? ☐ YES ☐ NO

FINAL THOUGHTS/INTERPRETATION:

THEME: **DATE:**

☐ FANTASY   ☐ SYMBOLIC

☐ NIGHTMARE   ☐ RANDOM

WHAT HAPPENED?

RECURRING? ☐ YES ☐ NO

FINAL THOUGHTS/INTERPRETATION:

THEME: **DATE:**

☐ FANTASY   ☐ SYMBOLIC

☐ NIGHTMARE   ☐ RANDOM

WHAT HAPPENED?

RECURRING? ☐ YES ☐ NO

FINAL THOUGHTS/INTERPRETATION:

THEME: **DATE:**

☐ FANTASY   ☐ SYMBOLIC

☐ NIGHTMARE   ☐ RANDOM

WHAT HAPPENED?

RECURRING? ☐ YES ☐ NO

FINAL THOUGHTS/INTERPRETATION:

THEME: **DATE:**

☐ FANTASY   ☐ SYMBOLIC

☐ NIGHTMARE ☐ RANDOM

WHAT HAPPENED?

RECURRING? ☐ YES ☐ NO

FINAL THOUGHTS/INTERPRETATION:

THEME: **DATE:**

☐ FANTASY   ☐ SYMBOLIC

☐ NIGHTMARE   ☐ RANDOM

WHAT HAPPENED?

RECURRING? ☐ YES ☐ NO

FINAL THOUGHTS/INTERPRETATION:

THEME: **DATE:**

☐ FANTASY   ☐ SYMBOLIC

☐ NIGHTMARE   ☐ RANDOM

WHAT HAPPENED?

RECURRING? ☐ YES ☐ NO

FINAL THOUGHTS/INTERPRETATION:

THEME: **DATE:**

☐ FANTASY   ☐ SYMBOLIC

☐ NIGHTMARE   ☐ RANDOM

WHAT HAPPENED?

RECURRING? ☐ YES ☐ NO

FINAL THOUGHTS/INTERPRETATION:

THEME: **DATE:**

☐ FANTASY   ☐ SYMBOLIC

☐ NIGHTMARE   ☐ RANDOM

WHAT HAPPENED?

RECURRING? ☐ YES ☐ NO

FINAL THOUGHTS/INTERPRETATION:

THEME: **DATE:**

☐ FANTASY   ☐ SYMBOLIC

☐ NIGHTMARE   ☐ RANDOM

WHAT HAPPENED?

RECURRING? ☐ YES ☐ NO

FINAL THOUGHTS/INTERPRETATION:

THEME: **DATE:**

☐ FANTASY   ☐ SYMBOLIC

☐ NIGHTMARE   ☐ RANDOM

WHAT HAPPENED?

RECURRING? ☐ YES ☐ NO

FINAL THOUGHTS/INTERPRETATION:

THEME: **DATE:**

☐ FANTASY   ☐ SYMBOLIC

☐ NIGHTMARE   ☐ RANDOM

WHAT HAPPENED?

RECURRING? ☐ YES ☐ NO

FINAL THOUGHTS/INTERPRETATION:

THEME: **DATE:**

- [ ] FANTASY
- [ ] SYMBOLIC
- [ ] NIGHTMARE
- [ ] RANDOM

WHAT HAPPENED?

RECURRING? [ ] YES [ ] NO

FINAL THOUGHTS/INTERPRETATION:

THEME: **DATE:**

☐ FANTASY   ☐ SYMBOLIC

☐ NIGHTMARE   ☐ RANDOM

WHAT HAPPENED?

RECURRING? ☐ YES ☐ NO

FINAL THOUGHTS/INTERPRETATION:

THEME: **DATE:**

☐ FANTASY   ☐ SYMBOLIC

☐ NIGHTMARE   ☐ RANDOM

WHAT HAPPENED?

RECURRING? ☐ YES ☐ NO

FINAL THOUGHTS/INTERPRETATION:

THEME: **DATE:**

☐ FANTASY   ☐ SYMBOLIC

☐ NIGHTMARE   ☐ RANDOM

WHAT HAPPENED?

RECURRING? ☐ YES ☐ NO

FINAL THOUGHTS/INTERPRETATION:

THEME: **DATE:**

☐ FANTASY   ☐ SYMBOLIC

☐ NIGHTMARE   ☐ RANDOM

WHAT HAPPENED?

RECURRING?   ☐ YES   ☐ NO

FINAL THOUGHTS/INTERPRETATION:

THEME: **DATE:**

☐ FANTASY   ☐ SYMBOLIC

☐ NIGHTMARE   ☐ RANDOM

WHAT HAPPENED?

RECURRING? ☐ YES ☐ NO

FINAL THOUGHTS/INTERPRETATION:

THEME: **DATE:**

☐ FANTASY   ☐ SYMBOLIC

☐ NIGHTMARE   ☐ RANDOM

WHAT HAPPENED?

RECURRING? ☐ YES ☐ NO

FINAL THOUGHTS/INTERPRETATION:

THEME: **DATE:**

☐ FANTASY   ☐ SYMBOLIC

☐ NIGHTMARE   ☐ RANDOM

WHAT HAPPENED?

RECURRING? ☐ YES ☐ NO

FINAL THOUGHTS/INTERPRETATION:

THEME: **DATE:**

☐ FANTASY   ☐ SYMBOLIC

☐ NIGHTMARE   ☐ RANDOM

WHAT HAPPENED?

RECURRING? ☐ YES ☐ NO

FINAL THOUGHTS/INTERPRETATION:

THEME: **DATE:**

☐ FANTASY   ☐ SYMBOLIC

☐ NIGHTMARE   ☐ RANDOM

WHAT HAPPENED?

RECURRING? ☐ YES ☐ NO

FINAL THOUGHTS/INTERPRETATION:

THEME: **DATE:**

☐ FANTASY   ☐ SYMBOLIC

☐ NIGHTMARE   ☐ RANDOM

WHAT HAPPENED?

RECURRING? ☐ YES ☐ NO

FINAL THOUGHTS/iNTERPRETATION:

THEME: **DATE:**

☐ FANTASY   ☐ SYMBOLIC

☐ NIGHTMARE   ☐ RANDOM

WHAT HAPPENED?

RECURRING? ☐ YES ☐ NO

FINAL THOUGHTS/INTERPRETATION:

THEME: **DATE:**

☐ FANTASY   ☐ SYMBOLIC

☐ NIGHTMARE   ☐ RANDOM

WHAT HAPPENED?

RECURRING? ☐ YES ☐ NO

FINAL THOUGHTS/INTERPRETATION:

THEME: **DATE:**

☐ FANTASY   ☐ SYMBOLIC

☐ NIGHTMARE   ☐ RANDOM

WHAT HAPPENED?

RECURRING? ☐ YES ☐ NO

FINAL THOUGHTS/INTERPRETATION:

THEME: **DATE:**

☐ FANTASY   ☐ SYMBOLIC

☐ NIGHTMARE   ☐ RANDOM

WHAT HAPPENED?

RECURRING? ☐ YES ☐ NO

FINAL THOUGHTS/INTERPRETATION:

THEME: **DATE:**

☐ FANTASY ☐ SYMBOLIC

☐ NIGHTMARE ☐ RANDOM

WHAT HAPPENED?

RECURRING? ☐ YES ☐ NO

FINAL THOUGHTS/INTERPRETATION:

THEME:　　　　　　　　　　**DATE:**

☐ FANTASY　　　☐ SYMBOLIC

☐ NIGHTMARE　　☐ RANDOM

WHAT HAPPENED?

RECURRING?　☐ YES　☐ NO

FINAL THOUGHTS/INTERPRETATION:

THEME: **DATE:**

☐ FANTASY   ☐ SYMBOLIC

☐ NIGHTMARE   ☐ RANDOM

WHAT HAPPENED?

RECURRING? ☐ YES ☐ NO

FINAL THOUGHTS/INTERPRETATION:

THEME: **DATE:**

☐ FANTASY   ☐ SYMBOLIC

☐ NIGHTMARE   ☐ RANDOM

WHAT HAPPENED?

RECURRING? ☐ YES ☐ NO

FINAL THOUGHTS/INTERPRETATION:

THEME: **DATE:**

☐ FANTASY   ☐ SYMBOLIC

☐ NIGHTMARE   ☐ RANDOM

WHAT HAPPENED?

RECURRING? ☐ YES ☐ NO

FINAL THOUGHTS/INTERPRETATION:

THEME: **DATE:**

☐ FANTASY   ☐ SYMBOLIC

☐ NIGHTMARE   ☐ RANDOM

WHAT HAPPENED?

RECURRING?   ☐ YES   ☐ NO

FINAL THOUGHTS/INTERPRETATION:

THEME: **DATE:**

☐ FANTASY   ☐ SYMBOLIC

☐ NIGHTMARE   ☐ RANDOM

WHAT HAPPENED?

RECURRING? ☐ YES ☐ NO

FINAL THOUGHTS/INTERPRETATION:

THEME: **DATE:**

☐ FANTASY   ☐ SYMBOLIC

☐ NIGHTMARE   ☐ RANDOM

WHAT HAPPENED?

RECURRING? ☐ YES ☐ NO

FINAL THOUGHTS/INTERPRETATION:

THEME: **DATE:**

☐ FANTASY   ☐ SYMBOLIC

☐ NIGHTMARE   ☐ RANDOM

WHAT HAPPENED?

RECURRING? ☐ YES ☐ NO

FINAL THOUGHTS/INTERPRETATION:

THEME: **DATE:**

☐ FANTASY   ☐ SYMBOLIC

☐ NIGHTMARE   ☐ RANDOM

WHAT HAPPENED?

RECURRING? ☐ YES ☐ NO

FINAL THOUGHTS/INTERPRETATION:

THEME: **DATE:**

☐ FANTASY   ☐ SYMBOLIC

☐ NIGHTMARE   ☐ RANDOM

WHAT HAPPENED?

RECURRING? ☐ YES ☐ NO

FINAL THOUGHTS/INTERPRETATION:

THEME: **DATE:**

☐ FANTASY   ☐ SYMBOLIC

☐ NIGHTMARE   ☐ RANDOM

WHAT HAPPENED?

RECURRING? ☐ YES ☐ NO

FINAL THOUGHTS/INTERPRETATION:

THEME: **DATE:**

☐ FANTASY   ☐ SYMBOLIC

☐ NIGHTMARE   ☐ RANDOM

WHAT HAPPENED?

RECURRING? ☐ YES ☐ NO

FINAL THOUGHTS/INTERPRETATION:

THEME: **DATE:**

☐ FANTASY   ☐ SYMBOLIC

☐ NIGHTMARE   ☐ RANDOM

WHAT HAPPENED?

RECURRING? ☐ YES ☐ NO

FINAL THOUGHTS/INTERPRETATION:

THEME: **DATE:**

- [ ] FANTASY   [ ] SYMBOLIC
- [ ] NIGHTMARE   [ ] RANDOM

WHAT HAPPENED?

RECURRING?   [ ] YES   [ ] NO

FINAL THOUGHTS/INTERPRETATION:

THEME: **DATE:**

☐ FANTASY   ☐ SYMBOLIC

☐ NIGHTMARE   ☐ RANDOM

WHAT HAPPENED?

RECURRING? ☐ YES ☐ NO

FINAL THOUGHTS/INTERPRETATION:

THEME: **DATE:**

☐ FANTASY   ☐ SYMBOLIC

☐ NIGHTMARE   ☐ RANDOM

WHAT HAPPENED?

RECURRING? ☐ YES ☐ NO

FINAL THOUGHTS/INTERPRETATION:

THEME: **DATE:**

☐ FANTASY   ☐ SYMBOLIC

☐ NIGHTMARE   ☐ RANDOM

WHAT HAPPENED?

RECURRING? ☐ YES ☐ NO

FINAL THOUGHTS/INTERPRETATION:

THEME: **DATE:**

☐ FANTASY ☐ SYMBOLIC

☐ NIGHTMARE ☐ RANDOM

WHAT HAPPENED?

RECURRING? ☐ YES ☐ NO

FINAL THOUGHTS/INTERPRETATION:

THEME: **DATE:**

☐ FANTASY   ☐ SYMBOLIC

☐ NIGHTMARE   ☐ RANDOM

WHAT HAPPENED?

RECURRING? ☐ YES ☐ NO

FINAL THOUGHTS/INTERPRETATION:

THEME: **DATE:**

☐ FANTASY   ☐ SYMBOLIC

☐ NIGHTMARE   ☐ RANDOM

WHAT HAPPENED?

RECURRING?   ☐ YES   ☐ NO

FINAL THOUGHTS/INTERPRETATION:

THEME: **DATE:**

☐ FANTASY   ☐ SYMBOLIC

☐ NIGHTMARE   ☐ RANDOM

WHAT HAPPENED?

RECURRING? ☐ YES ☐ NO

FINAL THOUGHTS/INTERPRETATION:

THEME:
                                            DATE:

☐ FANTASY   ☐ SYMBOLIC

☐ NIGHTMARE   ☐ RANDOM

WHAT HAPPENED?

RECURRING?   ☐ YES ☐ NO

FINAL THOUGHTS/INTERPRETATION:

THEME: **DATE:**

☐ FANTASY   ☐ SYMBOLIC

☐ NIGHTMARE   ☐ RANDOM

WHAT HAPPENED?

_____
_____
_____
_____
_____
_____
_____
_____
_____
_____
_____
_____
_____
_____
_____
_____
_____
_____
_____
_____
_____

RECURRING?   ☐ YES ☐ NO

FINAL THOUGHTS/INTERPRETATION:

THEME: **DATE:**

☐ FANTASY   ☐ SYMBOLIC

☐ NIGHTMARE   ☐ RANDOM

WHAT HAPPENED?

RECURRING? ☐ YES ☐ NO

FINAL THOUGHTS/INTERPRETATION:

THEME: **DATE:**

☐ FANTASY   ☐ SYMBOLIC

☐ NIGHTMARE   ☐ RANDOM

WHAT HAPPENED?

RECURRING? ☐ YES ☐ NO

FINAL THOUGHTS/INTERPRETATION:

THEME: DATE:

☐ FANTASY   ☐ SYMBOLIC

☐ NIGHTMARE   ☐ RANDOM

WHAT HAPPENED?

RECURRING? ☐ YES ☐ NO

FINAL THOUGHTS/INTERPRETATION:

THEME: **DATE:**

☐ FANTASY   ☐ SYMBOLIC

☐ NIGHTMARE   ☐ RANDOM

WHAT HAPPENED?

(blank ruled lines)

RECURRING? ☐ YES ☐ NO

FINAL THOUGHTS/INTERPRETATION:

THEME: **DATE:**

☐ FANTASY   ☐ SYMBOLIC

☐ NIGHTMARE   ☐ RANDOM

WHAT HAPPENED?

RECURRING? ☐ YES ☐ NO

FINAL THOUGHTS/INTERPRETATION:

THEME: **DATE:**

☐ FANTASY   ☐ SYMBOLIC

☐ NIGHTMARE   ☐ RANDOM

WHAT HAPPENED?

RECURRING?   ☐ YES   ☐ NO

FINAL THOUGHTS/INTERPRETATION:

Made in the USA
Las Vegas, NV
23 October 2024